DID YOU KNOW?

Wetland Series
V.2

Photos and Text by Maresa Pryor-Luzier

Front Cover: Sandhill Crane Colt

ISBN:979-8-9856138-0-3

Dedication

To my lovely granddaughters Faith & Harmony
May you always love the outdoors!

Tree Frogs

Toe Pads

How many tree frogs do you see?

Did you know there are many kinds of tree frogs throughout the world?

These five tree frogs need wet areas to lay their eggs, and all have toe pads to help them climb trees and walls.

What are toe pads? It is a circular disk on the end of their toes.

Tiger Salamander

What color are the spots on this Tiger Salamander?

Yellow.

Did you know salamanders are found near freshwater ponds or under wet logs? Usually after a rainstorm, early in the morning, and they also lay their eggs in the water.

Toad digging in

Spade for Digging

How long can a Spadefoot Toad live underground?

Did you know Spadefoot toads live underground for months at a time? They come to the surface after a heavy-heavy rainstorm.

What is a spade? A tool for digging.

They use their back foot like a spade to bring themselves to the surface or to go back underground. That's why they are called a spadefoot toad.

How are bird beaks/bills used?

Did you know bird bills or beaks are used in probing for food, eating seeds, catching fish, sipping nectar, trapping insects, and tearing food? All shaped to where they live.

Top left: Ibis bill probes food underneath the water.
Top Middle: Grosbeak eats seeds
Top Right: Pelican's bill catches fish
Lower Left: Hummingbird beak sips nectar
Middle: Woodpecker beak traps insects
Lower Right: Hawk beak tears food

How fast can a dragonfly fly?

Did you know they can fly up to 30 miles per hour while chasing flies and mosquitos?

Jack Rabbit

Cottontail Rabbit

How many types of wild Rabbits are there?

One.

Did you know a Jack Rabbit is a hare? Jack rabbits are much bigger and have **BIG** ears.

Cottontails are the true rabbit. They are smaller and found near water or grassy areas on the edge of an open meadow.

Honey Beehive

How do Bees keep their beehive cool from the summer heat?

Did you know honeybees collect water and bring it to the home or hive and spread the water across the eggs, and fan their wings to keep them cool? Just like an air conditioner.

Isn't that cool! (SMILE)

How many wildflowers do you see and what do they have in common?

Did you know these four wildflowers are all found in ponds or wet areas known as wetlands?

Which Butterfly is the Monarch?

How do Butterflies keep from becoming a meal?

Did you know Monarch caterpillars can only eat milkweed leaves? This makes the butterfly taste bad.

Another butterfly, the Queen butterfly copies the Monarch butterfly in color and looks. The bright orange colors signal a warning to others this butterfly is not for eating.

(The one on the left.)

How do Birds sing?

Did you know every bird has a voice box? This creates a series of sounds, like hello I'm happy, or warn others of danger.

How do Owls see at night?

Did you know Owls eyes are very sensitive to light? It's called "eyeshine." The reflective layer in the eye reflects light giving greater vision at night.

With Velvet

Without Velvet

How are Deer antlers formed?

Did you know male deer or bucks grow antlers each year? A small bone grows with a waxy, velvet covering. Just like a fingernail!

They shed or rub off the velvet exposing the hard surface of bone known as the antler.

Sandhill crane with colt

What do you call a baby Sandhill Crane?

Did you know a baby Sandhill Crane is called a colt just like a baby horse? They both have long legs and can run fast.

The name Sandhill comes from the Sandhills of the American Plains.

What do frogs, salamanders, deer, birds, flowers, and butterflies all have in common?

Did you know all living things need water? Wetlands provide a home, food, and water for wildlife and their young for future generations.

A wetland is a place sometimes flooded by water during the year. Next time you see a wetland, you will know what lives there . . .

Published world-wide, Maresa Pryor-Luzier has studied and photographed the natural world for most of her life. She was raised in Florida and now resides in New Mexico with her husband, Sadie the dog, a few kitties, miniature donkeys, and horses.

She speaks on photography, nature, and conservation. Her credits include magazine and books such as National Geographic, Ranger Rick, National Wildlife, and Audubon. Her next DYK book will be on the *"Rocky Mountain Series."*

Please let Maresa know what you thought about *Did You Know? Wetland Series* by leaving a short review on Amazon or your preferred online store. It will help other parents and children find her story. Thank you!

For more information or social media pages: https://www.maresapryorluzier.com
Facebook: https://www.facebook.com/mpluzierphotography
Instagram: https://www.instagram.com/mpluzier
Twitter: https://www.twitter.com/mpluzier

www.ingramcontent.com/pod-product-compliance
Lightning Source LLC
Chambersburg PA
CBHW061149030426
42335CB00003B/165